Y0-BQR-311

To Peg with my love,
Stan - Baipuli '53

ART OF INDIA

ART OF INDIA

AJIT MOOKERJEE

OXFORD BOOK & STATIONERY CO.

CALCUTTA   NEWDELHI   DARJEELING

TO SUDHA

PUBLISHED BY D. C. CHOPRA
LIMTON LIMITED, CALCUTTA-1

PRINTED IN INDIA
BY SREE SARASWATY PRESS LTD.
CALCUTTA-9

PREFACE

The spiritual and material aspects of Indian life are as significant as those of any other country—with its own sacrifice and understanding, achievement and frustration, toil and greed.

The sages of India found solace in meditation and tried to unfold the mysteries of the universe manifest in matter and energy, atoms and stars, and the people sweated and struggled for all that the world could give. They established kingdoms and empires; administered vast territories; produced generals and statesmen; artists and poets; musicians and mathematicians; philosophers and astronomers.

Their ships sailed across the oceans, and, in turn, from all over the world came traders in search of secret treasures.

Colonists from India moved to distant lands and established flourishing communities beyond the seas; their cultural missions crossed over snow-clad mountain peaks; their architects and artists made temples, statues and paintings of enduring strength and beauty.

A pilgrim journeying along the road of eternity will meet the monuments raising their spires and again falling into pieces, leaving only fragments to remind us of the departed glory. But the tradition remains unbroken : It is the great folk tradition that will continue to inspire our future generations for ages to come.

My thanks are due to Government of India, Department of Archaeology and Publications Division ; Calcutta University and Prof. D. P. Ghosh, Curator, Asutosh Museum ; Bharat Kala Bhawan, Banaras ; Indian Museum, Calcutta ; Victoria and Albert Museum, London ; and Johnston and Hoffmann, Calcutta, for giving permission to make use of copyright material. I have taken the greatest care to trace the owners of the photographs or other materials incorporated but should like to be forgiven in case any name has been omitted.

I am also grateful to Mr. Amiya Jiban Mookerjee, Mr. Samar Sen, Dr. Kalyan K. Ganguli and Mr. Jibapriya Guha for their valuable cooperation and particularly to Mr. Sudhansu Chowdhury for lending his photographs of Konarak.

A. M.

8

CONTENTS

APPROACH

BEYOND the highly civilized cities of Harappa and Mohenjo-daro in
the Indus valley, which flourished some five thousand years ago,
traces of palaeolithic and neolithic culture have been found
in many parts of India. The rock shelters of central and northern
India are now known to be the repositories of the earliest manifestation of pictorial art in this subcontinent. Standing out dimly upon
the rough walls of these caves are seen drawings of animals and men
generally representing hunting scenes and other group activities.
Numerous rock paintings discovered at Singanpur, Mirzapur,

Hoshangabad, etc., are strongly akin to the prehistoric cave paintings of Spain.

The hunting scene in Singanpur cave where a group of hunters is struggling to capture a bison is a forceful presentation in mauve, pale-yellow and burgundy-red. A similar scene in Mirzapur cave depicts the death agony of a wounded boar. Although many of these rock paintings are now unintelligible and superimposed by later drawings, enough is preserved to testify to the dynamic vision of the prehistoric artist.

Our knowledge, however, of this earliest art form, with all the fascination it offers, remains embryonic. But the art of the Indus valley is at once more familiar and comprehensive. The clear and coherent conceptions of plastic art which confront us for the first time at Harappa and Mohenjo-daro are undoubtedly the culmination of artistic traditions of centuries.

This was the turning point and with it Indian sculpture in the proper sense began. And it began with such a rich promise that René Grousset, while studying a Mohenjo-daro earthenware statuette of a seated monkey, remarks that 'it may well foreshadow the whole art of Indian animal sculpture, from the capitals of Asoka to the *ratha* of Mavalipuram'. It is not in animal forms alone that the art of the Indus valley anticipates the subsequent development of Indian sculpture. Among the many small fragments of sculpture so far discovered in these sites are figures of a dancer and a dancing girl and a small torso of plastic subtlety. These statuettes bear witness to the ease and certitude with which the artist of the Indus valley handled the

12

various plastic mediums like terracotta, ivory, bronze and alabaster.

Unlike their contemporaries in Egypt or Babylon, the Mohenjo-daro artists did not go in for the spectacular. They did not evolve a monumental art. No temples or palaces which point to a dominant kingship or priesthood have been found in the cities that have been explored. Perhaps social life and religious expression in the Indus valley civilization did not demand such art forms. But there are public baths, granaries, well constructed houses, wide thoroughfares and an intricate system of drainage which speak of an expansive and dignified civic life.

Art in the Indus valley, therefore, was conceived on a scale in which it could belong to the life of the people. The host of terracotta figurines, symbolic of a matriarchal culture, with their freshness of primeval joy, are representative of a folk tradition and link Mohenjo-daro with the prehistoric world. Most of the female figures centre round fertility. But in the absence of attributes, one does not know whether they stand for goddesses or human beings.

The mother and child group expresses a subconscious notion of the potential powers of woman. There is a total disregard for accuracy in anatomical details, but in each case the figurine is full of life, possessing a natural, quiet distinction, and a pride of fulfilment. The enigmatic expression of the mother gives her a feeling of a mysterious withdrawal, the rather compressed mouth and strong, queer, arched brows reveal an immobility which is the primeval root of all beauty. Another innate virtue of the primitive mind, sensitiveness to colour, expresses itself in endless varieties of illuminated potteries so abundantly found in Harappa and other Indus valley sites.

13

Of particular interest are the engravings on the seals that have been found in large numbers at Mohenjo-daro. The pictographic script which appears on some may eventually provide a clue to their use, but has not yet been deciphered. The subject of the engraving is usually an animal, the types most frequently represented being the humped or Brahmani bulls and unicorns. In the exquisite modelling of the bulls, the majesty and restrained vigour of the beast are strikingly conveyed. They are so successfully animated as to impart life into the figures which have otherwise a sphinx-like serenity.

Further, though sculpture of the human figure in the round has rarely survived, what has survived bears witness to the sense of volume characteristic of mature sculpture. This is illustrated at its best in the limestone statuette of a nude dancing figure from Harappa. The warm and lively body of a young male, revealing himself in contour, had never probably come so true in the medium of stone. Another illustration of this type can be found in a bronze statuette of a nude dancing girl from Mohenjo-daro. The sensitive moulding of her back, the tense poise of her legs, are most significant. 'But above all,' says Iqbal Singh, 'in the subtle comprehension of the dynamic expression which forms, as it were, an invisible background to her whole frame, plastic representation achieves a quality of perfection hardly surpassed even by the medieval South Indian bronzes'.

This period is further marked by the emergence of phallic emblems, which indicated a growing male awareness that the source of generative power is the father, so long regarded as just a 'way-opener'. The discovery that male semen impregnates the female provided an important basis for the rise of the phallic cult not only in India but

14

most probably throughout the world. Even an anthropomorphic representation appears to be embodied in the figures of Pasupatinatha seated in a yogi pose, found at Mohenjo-daro, which is probably a direct predecessor of the later popular and powerful deity, Siva, whose cult is closely associated with that of the lingam.

The Indus civilization did not collapse, as we commonly think, sometime about 2000 B.C., but was assimilated in successive stages of Indian life and thought. Although aesthetic history during the following fifteen centuries remains shrouded in mystery and our lack of knowledge about any archaeological store of this period may be unfortunate, the people who dwelt in India during those centuries were certainly no idlers.

Vedic burial-mounds, which may be placed round 800 B.C. or thereabout, at Lauriya-Nandangarh and other places have yielded, among various objects, a small gold plaque bearing the figure of a nude female, probably the earth goddess mentioned in the burial hymns. A few more terracotta figurines of similar antiquity have also been found at Taxila, Bhita and other sites. The technique of execution is the same as in the Indus valley and the figurines have a close affinity which suggests a continuity in art traditions. Though very few in number, they are of vital significance in so far as they provide the only link between the products of proto-historic age and the subsequent periods.

Literary evidence shows that the Vedic people were also experimenting with symbolic expressions that bore the transcendental excellence of their thought and emotion. Their attainment in meditative philosophy stands out even today as the finest ever achieved by man. For instance, the Rig Veda, the oldest Hindu scripture compiled as early as 1500 B.C., reveals a knowledge of the awakening of the human soul and its eternal inquiries into the mysteries of the universe.

This has been intensified in the Upanishads which in a masterly way analyse the divinity and the destiny of the soul, its evolution through a process of searching towards the ultimate reality and the merging into it of life and death, of energy and substance.

In the world of contemplation the Vedic people were soaring high and their experiments in art expression became as universal as their profound questions. In this approach, "the cry of 'Not this! Not that!' which echoes so frequently in the Upanishads, is a confession not of ignorance, but of the breakdown of human language before the memory of that experience." Art became symbolic with their vertical and horizontal lines, dots and circles conceived almost in spiritual dimension.

Throughout these periods, the fertility figurines following the Mohenjo-daro tradition continued to furnish the dominant motif. But the representation gradually tended to become archaic and stiff. It is only with the growth of Buddhism into a great popular religious movement that a comprehensive tradition of visual art emerged.

We must look upon the Buddhist art pattern as a whole. An extraordinary variety of contradictory and conflicting elements enters into the texture of this pattern. There are, to begin with, Asoka's capitals on the one hand and reliefs of Bharhut and Sanchi on the other. These sculptures show the impress of two divergent techniques. The reliefs of Bharhut and Sanchi were derived from the indigenous tradition of wood and ivory carving, whereas the other was a comparatively stylized continuation from the early realism and as such an 'aftermath of the Indus valley'.

The Mauryan Empire flourished under Asoka during the third century B.C. Asoka's propagation of the Rule of Law followed his adoption of Buddhism as a State religion. Edicts of his imperial policy were conveyed through monolithic stone pillars, specimens of which have come down in well preserved state. These columns of highly polished white sandstone are designed to stand by themselves without any architectural relation to their environment. The sheer columns rising up to forty feet or so are surmounted by capitals crowned with animated figures, lions being the most frequent. The well known lion capital of Sarnath, one of the finest specimens, portrays the animal with striking realism and dignity. In spite of their artistic significance, the popular appeal of these capitals was limited owing to the didactic nature of their application.

A few large sculptures in the round, on the other hand, of a folk tradition that have survived can be placed in or before the Mauryan period. The material employed in all these examples is grey sandstone of a type similar to that used for the Asokan capitals. Equally significant is a small fragment of the same period portraying a weeping woman. The attitude of the figure, while singling out her individuality and dignity, makes her a universal symbol of sorrow rather than an episode from history. Though conceived in a limited space, the figure in relief somehow reproduces the massive grandeur which characterizes her contemporaries. The colossal standing female figure from Besnagar as well as a male torso from Baroda near

Parkham have obviously the same tradition as the Didarganj Yakshi figure commonly known as the chauri-bearer. In conception as well as execution, this figure is characterized by massive roundness which is almost 'brutal in its affirmation' of a physical energy 'not yet spiritualized'. The specific purpose for which she was carved still remains a mystery—she stands however as a symbol of unity between the regal and eternal. She is folk-lore, making life stir until one's blood runs warmer and quicker.

This warmth bursts into life immediately after Asoka, during the second century B.C., in the sculptured gateway and railings of Bharhut. The art of Bharhut is a popular art, an art appealing to and drawing its inspiration from the people. It seeks to help the common man find his position in the system of life in terms of values of his own existence. The scenes, therefore, derive their motifs from woods, fields and streams that surrounded the village folk. Instead of the majestic lions of the Asokan capitals, there are familiar animals of the Indian scene. In the carvings of the Yakshas and the Nagas, the fertility goddesses of the village and the spirits of woods and streams, in whom the simple people believed, the guild artists of Bharhut were anticipating a psychological reality that was to receive its justification only in our own age.

A century later comes the stupa of Sanchi, with its magnificent gateways, even richer in ornament and invention than Bharhut. Although it follows the tradition of Bharhut, the Sanchi carvings show a definite sculptural advance. The figures are brought out in deeper light and shade. The primitive quality of Bharhut is gradually abandoned to impart a new spirit to the movement. The diversity

18

of Jataka stories is restricted and though the friendly spirits of woods and streams reappear, they lose their familiar identity. The rendering on the whole attains an epic character away from introspection and simplicity.

Roughly contemporaneous with Sanchi are the rock-cut chaitya caves of Western India—the best known examples being those at Bhaja, Nasik and Karli near Poona. Hewn out of living rock these caves are apparently efforts to impart for the first time a stability to the architectural pattern hitherto practised in wood and other perishable material.

The sculpture panels associated with these chaitya halls derived inspiration from sources which had been responsible for the creation of the railing sculpture at Bodhgaya, a sculpture of massive corporeality.

The duality of formal expression that we find in sculptures since the days of Asoka is apparent in Buddhism as well. The spiritual upsurge is trying to find expression through symbols, but at the same time, it is the triumph of life in all its material manifestation that is expressed through the lovingly moulded contours of the dryads of Sanchi or the maidens of Mathura. And there are the frescoes on the walls of Ajanta caves, 'that pictorial panorama with its endless lyrical dreams and phantasies of the mystery of the female flesh and its promise of bliss.'

The climax of the dual aspect may be witnessed at Amaravati, where in the second century A.D., 'the most voluptuous and delicate flower of Indian sculpture' was produced. The main interest, however, is concentrated on the medallions and panelled friezes which have as their themes stories of the birth and life of the Buddha. A design more complex in composition than anything produced so far distinguishes them and the supple carvings throb with a new linear rhythm destined to be developed more fully later. Two lines of carved stone slabs, 160 and 162 feet respectively in diameter, formed something like a wainscot round the stupas and the area of carving on the railing was 1700 sq. ft. Mainly in the bas-relief tradition of Bharhut and Bodhgaya, they also incorporate some of the new features already noted in the sculptures at Mathura and Gandhara.

Following the same line of tradition, the craftsman of Mathura produced, from local material, graceful but highly sensuous figures during the first three centuries A.D. Here, the adaptation or transformation of sculpture to domestic needs came indeed as a silent revolution, and this sculpture had equally strong, religious and domestic bearings. Most of the Mathura figures are not only three-dimensional, but have dynamic characteristics in that they make the spectators move round them for a complete grasp. The technique as employed here has, again, a strong influence of indigenous clay-modelling, giving the impression of 'clay transmuted into stone'.

The important feature of the Mathura 'school' was the creation of an iconography which evolved through the portrayal of the Bodhisattvas and the Buddha, and the Jain Tirthamkaras.

The solidity and massiveness represented in the Buddha images are in interesting contrast with the numerous happy female figures—in company of birds, flowers, trees and flowing streams, mostly carved on railing pillars—'who stand', in the words of an ancient Indian writer, 'in delicate poses and sportive attitudes with nimble waists and firm breasts, stealing the hearts of gods and men as it were with their teasing glances.'

These Yakshinis—the glamour girls of Mathura—are typical examples of grace, charm and energy of youth revealed in stone.

While we find the Mathura style, notably in ivory carvings, spread beyond the boundaries of India, especially to Begram in Afghanistan and as far as Pompeii in Italy, the north-western border province, known as Gandhara, with its capital at Taxila, had already a hybrid art which was 'more interesting than beautiful'.

Gandhara sculptures, with their varying qualities, were in the service of Buddhism ; but in the absence of any date in the thousands of images discovered so far it has been hard to determine their correct chronological sequence ; nor does their style give any clue in that direction.

'Tachose schist', a grey slate, was usually the material used for the carving of images. Huge Buddha statues, the largest being over 175 feet in height, have been carved in stone in the rocks of Bamiyan—a place dotted with Buddhist caves and monasteries. In the composition of these figures, lime was used where stone was not available and castings of the faces in moulds and plastering of the bodies by the 'stick-and-rag' technique were adopted. Innumerable images in the Hadda area serve as an example.

There is a controversy over the influence of Gandhara sculpture on the development of the Buddhist and the Jain images. Were the Gandhara and the Mathura types produced simultaneously? Coomaraswamy answers in the affirmative, and holds that they were done 'in the middle or near the beginning of the first century A.D., and that only after the local types had been established did each affect the other.'

Gandhara art however remains stereotyped and commonplace in the art world of India.

The Gupta period that followed saw the culmination of the creative efforts made hitherto and of the reorganization of all earlier experiments and experiences. For the first time, the political, social, cultural and economic life of the country crystallized into a definite pattern and art also synchronized with this process. The formulae of aesthetic taste were established and various shastric injunctions followed. But instead of geometrical measurements, Gupta sculptures were expressed in curves found in the rhythm of nature. No realistic delineation of anatomy was allowed, joints and bones were hidden and eternal youth had to be expressed through softly rounded limbs and placidly smooth faces. Art became sophisticatedly naïve.

During this period the Buddha image was fully evolved ; its essential purpose was to satisfy a spiritual urge. The benign and compassionate face, the exquisitely beautiful gestures or mudras in hands—'giving', 'blessing', 'reassuring', 'teaching', 'renouncing'—all conveyed the spiritual message to the afflicted world. The sculptures tended towards abstraction—flesh becoming spirit, human form passing into divinity.

This was in fact an echo of the conception of the Upanishads, where man was regarded 'not as a creature of the natural world, but as the vehicle of expression of an immortal and changeless spirit, the Atman'. Very likely this abstraction was directly responsible for the creation of the multi-armed and multi-headed images in India, and those artists known as the silpi-yogins, in order to bring out the picture of the fuller reality that underlies the bodily form and movement, had to subject themselves to a strict spiritual discipline. This humility showed the desire of the artist to be in communion with the universal spirit. The classical quality of the Dhyani Buddhas, typical examples of this, provided inspiration for the later forms both in India and beyond her mountains and seas.

A high standard of technical and artistic efficiency was also found in the art of metal casting, notably in the colossal copper images of the Buddha. One of the best known examples is the impressive, standing Buddha figure from Sultanganj, cast by *cire-perdue* process and assembled in sections. Another interesting feature of this period is the terracotta art portraying mostly Brahmanical divinities found abundantly at Ahichchhatra, Basarh, Set-mahet, Rajghat, etc. These figures are evidence of a popular tradition, unaffected by scholastic and literary conventions.

Most of the classical paintings belonging to the Gupta period have survived the ravages of time. While certain Ajanta murals which can be traced back as early as 2nd century B.C. have dimmed almost beyond recognition, those drawn during the late Gupta period (450-600 A.D.) are mostly intact with all their glory and grandeur. Apparently Ajanta murals depict the Jataka or the Buddha's birth stories but these represent the entire force of life in terms of phenomena and romances.

The magnificence of observation and the grouping of animal life, and the composition of human figures in architectural settings found on the walls of Ajanta has been enhanced by a colour work, the base of which has been served by layers of mud, straw and plaster. Skilful gradation of tone in bringing out the highlights and volume, efforts in aerial perspective and a mastery of the relation of forms in line and colour are some of the salient features of the murals of Ajanta.

The planning of the halls of Ajanta, hewn out from living rock, is done in such a manner as to make each element of colour, form and line progress towards a climax as it leads to the central cell flanked by the paintings of 'Beautiful Bodhisattvas'. The Buddha image is reached finally—stone brought to life in colour. All storms of the human heart are silenced before it in an echo of nirvana or renunciation.

No tale is told on the ceilings which are covered with intricate geometric designs. The masters responsible for the execution of these must have been well up in interior decoration for generations. The way they have maintained unity in variety and arranged low relief, ornamental carvings and masses of pillars, etc. in keeping with the architectural structures of the caves, truly speaks of their unsurpassed ability and ingenuity.

24

The graceful and festive damsels, the lovely Apsaras, with fully blossomed life 'bursting through the moon-breasts and wine-jar-heaps'—are yet another scene that attracts one's wistful attention. Human from first to last—they fly, they dance, they court, they 'make love unabashed'.

Life in all its aspects was manifest to a high degree in these paintings and sculptures as well as in music, dance and drama. But a formal classification and codification of almost all arts and social patterns, as evidenced through various literary works, took place during this period. The classical rigidity of the Gupta aristocracy was slowly being engulfed by a powerful mythology that steadily paved the way for a revolutionary change.

True, Buddhism, as a cultural force, predominated for several centuries since the days of Asoka; but a growing movement that foreshadowed the Brahmanical revival determined its reorientation at almost every crucial stage.

Under the Palas in Bengal, the Mahayana form of Buddhism replaced the rigid Hinayana school, revitalizing the classical phase of Indian art for the time being, but it was only a conventionalized repetition of originally noble forms.

Buddhism had been losing its hold on its birth-place but its influence was profoundly felt by the world outside. Countries far beyond the Indo-Gangetic plain pulsated with inspiration, and Indian art, particularly of this period and that which followed immediately, with all its charm and dignity, found a new home in Tun Huang and Lung-men in the distant lands of Central Asia, beyond the coast line of China and Korea, in the Horyuji temple at Nara in Japan; in the cave carvings of Bamiyan and Hadda on the borders of Afghanistan, the cities of Kashgar, Yarkand and Khotan; in the murals of Sigiriya in Ceylon, temples of Pagan in Burma; guilded shrines of Siam and Angkors in Cambodia; again in the gigantic stupa of Borobudur in Java.

By the end of the Gupta period, it must have been evident that the 'ultimate supremacy of Vedantism was only a matter of time'.

Buddhism was gradually losing its initiative, and sculptors were 'abandoning the image of the silent and static Buddha to offer homage to more restless and dynamic deities'. Buddhism itself became more and more Brahmanical until it eventually lost its character as an independent movement, Buddha himself being assimilated into the medieval Brahmanic pantheon as the incarnation of the Hindu god, Vishnu.

Aesthetically, although not realized all at once, the change effected by Brahmanism came with immense plastic possibilities in a new universe of imagery. With certain basic qualities intact in apparent variations, Brahmanical art has given us so many images and forms—now monstrous and sublime, now grotesque and delicate, abstract and sensual—as never attempted before by any other art.

In seeming chaos and confusion, we find in Brahmanical art a sense of broad symphonic order—a joy of rhythm. The profusion that creates an impression of bewilderment soon fades into the exuberance of nature that pervades this art. This is experienced in the Descent of the Ganges of Mahabalipuram. The large number of figures carved out of solid rock 'with apparent disregard of all rational composition is seen on closer examination to radiate from and conveyed towards a central axis in its timeless descent.'

Between the profound stillness of the central head of the Mahesvaramurti of the Elephanta cave and the dynamic poise of Nataraja of South India, we have again modulations, subtle and unique, representing the most characteristic phases of the art of this period.

The sculptures of Elura cave are so full of vitality as to overwhelm the visitor at each successive step. The Kailasa temple which, for instance, is cut, carved and sculptured from virgin rock as the artists progressed from the top downwards—stands with all its stupendous magnificence as a unique achievement. About 200,000 tons of solid stone are known to have been removed in chiselling out this Siva temple.

This rhythm of Brahmanical art finds its counterpart in the economic significance of medieval feudalism. Many divergent religious thoughts and emotions coexisted and were tolerated in the broad-based social order. Sculptors reacted to these cross-currents with a futuristic adoption of many-headed and many-handed figures, representing rapidity of movement and change. In the realm of plastic art we are confronted with a grandeur of conception magnificently realized in the images of Siva and Parvati, Nataraja and Ardhanarisvara. The image of Ardhanarisvara, symbolizing the union of the male and female principles that are creative without antithesis, has the poise of detached calm and yet shows all the vitality of biological existence. The symbolic representation of Nataraja, on the other hand, as the essence of cosmic transformation of energy into mass and of mass into energy has all the rapture of bliss and realization. The dance, as it were, manifests the eternal existence of human aspiration in the ever-changing world of space and time.

In the creation of this panorama of 'gods and goddesses' the artist cared little to express his own individuality. His creation yet turned out occasionally to be a complete departure—a rare phenomenon

27

in Indian art. The artist never sought to immortalize himself through his art, and in his creation he completely lost his own identity. But in these rare departures—as we find in the so-called goddess Ganga—he brings her down to the level of an earthly mortal, as it were, and gives her all the qualities and tenderness of an ordinary human being. He makes his goddess human out and out, 'deep in all the heat of the pondering female blood, the female urge, the female nature', and enlivens her as a 'young girl of unsurpassing loveliness'.

The sculptures of this period, however, form part of the architectural design, and the temple background in which these were set had a significance of its own. Detached from this background these sculptures lose much of their meaning. That is why in a museum, without the spirit, setting, and psychology so clearly associated with them, the understanding or appreciation of Indian sculpture becomes poor and inadequate.

From the 6th century A.D. caves gave place gradually to structural temple building. The horizontal and domed tops changed into vertical and pointed. The vertically set sculptures helped not only the upward thrust of the medieval temples, but had a decorative effect 'with a pronounced feeling for volume, perhaps foreshadowing a change in the medium of expression'.

However, no perspective of Brahmanical art would be complete without its overpowering sensuous quality being taken into account. In the reliefs of the temples of Konarak and Khajuraho, the sensual element is developed to its logical culmination, to a point where it has almost completely shattered the aesthetic barriers and forced the ultimate realization that life is art. What is justified and fundamental in life must also be justified and fundamental in art. It is no longer a question of that 'provocative indulgence' of the female figures from which Roger Fry recoils with puritanical shudder. Here we are confronted with erotic ecstasy in all its plastic possibilities. The love-plays (*bandhas*) of these images rouse a baffling query in the western mind but to an Indian observer the motive is simple and clear. In the world a man and a woman unite. Nothing is so true in terms of life as the after-glow of a happy union. These mating figures are drawn together in productive forces towards the creation of new life, new dynamic forms. Filled with the sense of ecstatic conviction, they are no longer torn between the contradiction of life and social existence.

These released forces militated against the interest of the ruling class which was now strongly entrenched at the termination of the expansive phase of feudalism. A cry of artistic formalism and aesthetic injunction was therefore raised throughout the country in order to damp and clamp down the creative movement. The result was an orgy of bombastic ornamentation and hysterical tendency towards flatulent magnificence so vivid in the temples of Mount Abu, Belur, Halebid or in the gopurams of South India.

Art declined. And for the first time in recorded history, India faced during this period a system of strange contrast with the advent of Islam. Out of the conflict arose problems which it was the task of Indian culture to solve. New religious and philosophical thoughts were evolved to mark the rapprochement between the Hindu and Moslem outlook. After the initial impact the Moslem ruling class ceased to be foreigners. This reaction to the Indian environment was reflected in the development of the artistic tradition of the next few centuries.

In the architecture of northern India, the general principle undergoes an almost revolutionary change. Hindu and Moslem elements merged to produce this form. Where the fusion is complete, we have brilliant architectural expression. Akbar's Fatehpur Sikri brings together these elements with the confidence of an empire builder and anticipates the more sophisticated monument where Mumtaj sleeps under the most beautiful and expensive memorial in the world. The Taj Mahal is a wonder in architectural creation. The painting which was brought to India by Babur, the founder of the Mughal Empire, was likewise intensely individualistic and sophisticated. It was not interested in crowds or masses. The stamp of individualism reached exaggerated length and reduced painting to mere portraiture, where characters 'are not characters at all, but photographs out of focus'. Wherever this luxury of Mughal Court art came in contact with the popular tradition, it produced that sophistication which is evident in the Rajput or Kangra paintings.

The mythology that once existed as a link between the economic and spiritual structures of society was no longer powerful enough to resist the unholy alliance between the ruling cliques. The result was that the indigenous vigour of Rajput tradition was dulled by a tendency towards archaic sensuality, even sexuality and idle romanticism, which had the patronage of the princes and emperors who were sufficiently well off to devote their leisure to the enjoyment of this art form.

Even the Jain miniatures, which had long retained their boldness also showed 'the tormented outlines of faces at once nervous and sensual, representations of human beings whose passage through life is made difficult by the awareness of fears that belong to an age of conformity which is also on the threshold of the Reformation'.

When individualism decayed into selfishness, the Indian aristocracy was in the process of disintegration. Public life had been reduced to systematic pillage, and the attitude towards life was extremely artificial and had no roots in everyday existence. The cult of beauty, 'art for art's sake', was practised as a form of escapism. All interests centred round the sentimental romances, which were endlessly repeated in both painting and poetry, and fictitious portraits of sultanas, begums and ranis. They were dream figures of idealized feminine beauty and accomplishment, delicately made up, decked out in the finest dresses and over-loaded with jewellery. This cult resembled the cult of the ballerina in France of the rococo period, when kings and princes lay at the feet of the adored.

But out of the dead remains of these court splendours there finally arose a cultural awakening of the Indian masses. This was a period of constant revolt against the conventional fetters of social and religious ideas. Chandidas, the greatest popular composer of Padavali songs, declared in the 15th century:

> "Listen, O brother man, the Truth of Man is the
> highest of truths; there is no other truth above it."

Gods tremble before men, ready to do the biddings of the peasant, to plough his field, harvest his crop and carry it to his home. A large number of newly discovered folk paintings portray the real conditions of the people's life at that time, and every one of these paintings is a condemnation of the social injustice. At the bottom of each scroll there are always scenes of Hell depicting every imaginable torture to which all anti-social elements are subjected in punishment of their worldly sins. In order to leave no doubt in the popular mind about the real meaning of these paintings, explanatory songs composed by the artists themselves always accompanied the public unrolling of the scrolls.

Their usual themes are street scenes, popular folk-lore, festivals and family re-unions, the joys and sorrows of everyday life together with biting satires on the vices of the decaying social order. Apart from its simple technique, Indian folk art by its nature and function, has useful lessons for creative artists in search of basic forms.

It is not a coincidence that the same basic forms run through the artistic expression of the few surviving tribes who still maintain a more or less primitive way of life. The plastic freedom has been kept alive in the wood carvings of Maria Gond tribes of Bastar State and particularly among the Nagas of Eastern India. The mind which expresses itself in direct simplicity and vigour of primitive art was poignantly brought out when a Naga youth, asked about his trouble, replied at once: 'Whenever I love a girl, she immediately becomes pregnant'. The thrust of his chisel has the same certainty and boldness.

Until recently nobody has taken the trouble of recording the artistic tradition of these people. The impact of Europe brought in an entirely new set of conditions which upset the social basis of primitive and folk art tradition of India. Even a century ago, the life of the guild artist was closely integrated in the economic life of

32

the village. In exchange of his art products the artist was assigned a measure of land by the village community for his maintenance. Thus the other party to the deal was the collective organization of the village and the artist was primarily an artist of the people. But with the break-up of the economic life of the villages that followed the British rule, the indigenous arts and crafts were not only seriously threatened but destroyed in many parts of the country.

The Europeans who came to India had no intention of settling here and were not really interested in a cultural synthesis between the East and the West. It was as if two closed systems faced each other and were not prepared either to influence or to imbibe anything from the contact. Nor was there any attempt to build up a new integration though there were sporadic efforts by a few western scholars who had been dazzled by the splendour of Indian civilization. The spirit of European art on the other hand could not be successfully assimilated by the Indian artists in their blind imitation. The result was Ravi Varma, whose syrupy pictures were an extreme example of philistine perversity.

But the period of fake European tradition did not last long. The wave of reformism, particularly in Bengal, needed a new vehicle of artistic expression. The rising Indian bourgeoisie took to classicism which was introduced by Abanindranath Tagore and carried all over India by his students. The outcome of this movement is well known as the Bengal School of Art in which the name of Nandalal Bose stands out. He depicted the mythological stories in the traditional technique of the Ajanta mural paintings. The enthusiasm for antiquity was surely the ideological reflection of the struggle over the choice of technique, western or eastern. The enthusiasm continued until the economic crisis of World War I, which sharpened the Indian national movement and led to the growth of mass organizations, and brought new trends. All the artifices of the old school, now of no use to any class, were no longer appropriate to the aspirations and aesthetic tendencies produced by the modern social relationships.

In the period that followed, Rabindranath Tagore took up painting. Inspired by modern thought and technique, the daring experiment of Tagore marks the final break with the sentimental love for artistic revivalism. The dramatic appearance of Jamini Roy as a popular artist is a direct outcome of this departure. Today the name of Jamini Roy can be placed side by side with those of Cézanne, Picasso or Matisse. Like many who have broken with conventions in their quest for new sources of inspiration, Jamini Roy is sustained by the art of the people, which is ageless and universal.

CHRONOLOGY

PALAEOLITHIC: Hand-axes, scrapers, flints, knives, etc., from Kashmir, Mayurbhanj, Guntur, Nellore, Cuddapah, Kurnool and some parts of Madhya Pradesh.

NEOLITHIC: Celts, ring-stones, hammer-stones from Chotanagpur, Orissa, Bengal and Assam. Cave paintings of Madhya Pradesh and Uttar Pradesh, notably at Singanpur, Hoshangabad and Mirzapur.

MEGALITHIC: Dolmens, menhirs, cromlechs, burial jars and mounds in Sind, South and Western India. Dravidian civilization.

c. 3000-1500 B.C. INDUS VALLEY CULTURE: Steatite seals and

bronze figures, jewellery, painted pottery, terracotta figurines from Harappa, Mohenjo-daro, Chanhu-daro, etc.

c. 1500 B.C. ARYAN SETTLEMENT: 1500 B.C. Rig Veda, c. 800 B.C. Earth Goddess and Vedic burial mounds, etc. from Lauriya-Nandangarh and Bhita. 800 B.C. Upanishads.

c. 642 B.C. SAISUNAGA DYNASTY: Mahavira 599-527 B.C., Buddha 563-483 B.C., Jataka stories 500-200 B.C.

322-185 B.C. MAURYA DYNASTY: Yaksha figures, black pottery, terracotta figurines from Patna, Basarh, Set-Mahet, etc.

272-232 B.C. ASOKA: Monolithic pillars, rock-edicts, early cave architecture.

185-28 B.C. SUNGA AND KANVA DYNASTIES: Sculptured gateways and railings of Bharhut, Sanchi and Bodhgaya.

c. 60 B.C.-48 A.D. PARTHIAN AND SAKA DYNASTIES: Early Gandhara sculptures.

c. 30-250 A.D. KUSHAN DYNASTY: Mathura sculptures. Origin of the Buddha image. 67 A.D. Buddhism reaches China.

230 B.C.-225 A.D. ANDHRA DYNASTY: Sculptured stupas at Amaravati and Nagarjuni-kunda. Clay figures from Kundapur.

320-600 A.D. GUPTA DYNASTY: Golden Age of Indian art and literature. Main centres of sculpture Mathura and Sarnath. Stone and brick temples at Deogarh, Bhitargaon, etc. Murals at Ajanta and Bagh, contemporary murals at Sigiriya, Ceylon ; Bamiyan, Afghanistan ; and Tun Huang, Central Asia.

7TH-10TH CENTURY A.D. EARLY MEDIEVAL PERIOD: Pallava Dynasty, c. 325-700 A.D. Rock-cut shrines and sculptures at Mahabalipuram. Chalukya Dynasty, 550-642 A.D. Temples at Badami and

Aihole. Rashtrakuta Dynasty, 757-973 A.D. Kailasa temple and murals at Elura; cave temple at Elephanta. Pala Dynasty, c. 750-1100 A.D. Stone and metal sculptures and illustrated manuscripts. Sculptors: Dhiman and Bitpalo.

8TH-10TH CENTURY A.D. INDIAN ART ABROAD: Borobudur and Prambanam in Java. Angkor Wat and Angkor Thom in Cambodia. Hindu rule in East Java, 10th to 16th century A.D. Temples at Pagan in Burma. Thousand Buddhas in Lung-men caves in China. Horyuji temple at Nara in Japan.

11TH-13TH CENTURY A.D. LATE MEDIEVAL PERIOD: Temples at Khajuraho. Solankis of Gujarat, 765-1197 A.D. Jain temples at Mount Abu, Girnar, etc. Eastern Gangas of Orissa, 1076-1148 A.D. Temples at Bhuvanesvar, Konarak, and Puri. Chola Dynasty, 907-1053 A.D. Temples at Tanjore, South Indian bronzes, images of Nataraja. Hoysala and Yadava Dynasties, 1111-1318 A.D. Temples at Halebid and Belur.

1206-1526 A.D. SULTANATE OF DELHI: Early Indo-Islamic architecture.

1526-1802 A.D. MUGHAL EMPIRE: Mughal architecture at Delhi, Agra, Fatehpur Sikri, Allahabad, etc. Mughal gardens at Lahore and Srinagar. Mughal paintings 17th to 19th century A.D. Rajput and Pahari paintings.

18TH-20TH CENTURY A.D. BRITISH PERIOD: Archaeological Survey of India. Folk arts and crafts and primitive survivals. Bengal School, Abanindranath Tagore, Nandalal Bose. Jamini Roy.

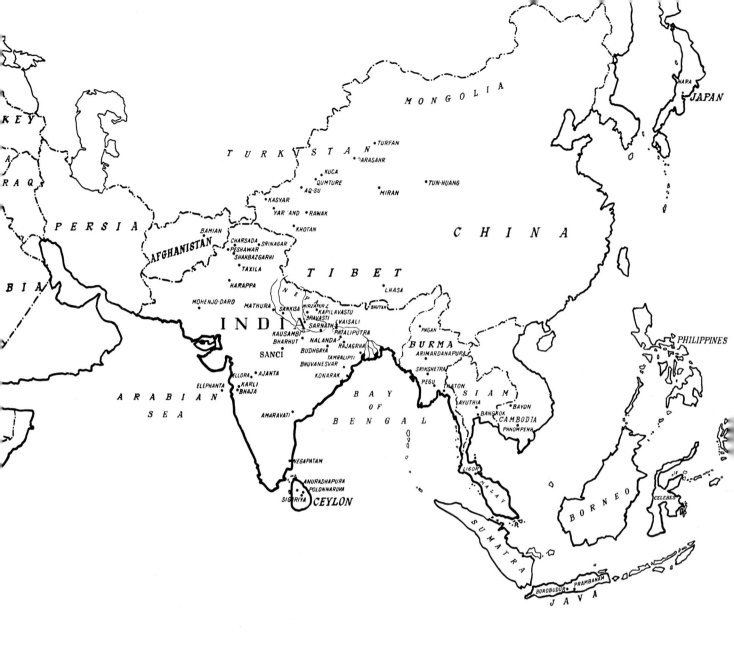

In India we find during every period when her civilization
bloomed, an intense joy in life and nature, a pleasure in the act
of living, the development of art and music and literature and
song and dancing and painting and the theatre, and even a highly
sophisticated inquiry into sex relations.

JAWAHARLAL NEHRU

2 ABOVE
WOUNDED BOAR
Rock painting, mauve, pale-yellow and burgundy-red
Date : End of the Old Stone Age in India
Location : Mirzapur, Uttar Pradesh
The boar portraying the agony of death shows the primitive man's triumph over his adversaries in the animal world. The depth and modelling have considerably added to the aesthetic value.

1 LEFT
HUNTING SCENE
Rock painting, mauve, pale-yellow and burgundy-red
Date : End of the Old Stone Age in India
Location : Singanpur, Madhya Pradesh
Some of the drawings represent men and animals gripped in intense struggle. While dealing with the period 20,000-10,000 B.C. it is difficult to assume whether each of these drawings had magical significance or existed independent of it.

3 LEFT
MALE DANCER, Harappa, W. Punjab
Grey limestone, 10 cm. high
Date : c. 3000-2000 B.C.
Location : Archaeological Museum,
Harappa
With the left leg thrown in a swing and
the body half turned, the figure shows
the sculptor's mastery over his material.
The head, arms and the genitals, all
now missing, were socketed into the
torso. Cement was used to fix the
nipples.

4 RIGHT
TORSO, Harappa, W. Punjab
Red limestone, 9 cm. high
Date : c. 3000-2000 B.C.
Location : Archaeological Museum,
Harappa
Extraordinarily exact in anatomical
detail, the male torso shows both
volume and suppleness foreshadowing
the Gangetic art, especially of the
Mauryan age. Main feature of the
technique is the socketing of head and
arms. Nipples were separately fixed.

5 ABOVE
SEAL, Mohenjo-daro, Sind
Location : Archaeological Museum, Mohenjo-daro
Intaglioed without any trace of previously drawn outline, this representation of the bull shows a remarkable advance in craftsmanship. The pictograph at the top is yet undeciphered.

Steatite, 3·8 × 3·8 cm.
Date : c. 3000-2000 B.C.

6 RIGHT BELOW
FIGURINE, Mohenjo-daro, Sind
Location : Archaeological Museum, Mohenjo-daro
The bejewelled figurine probably represents a sophisticated female. The body with accentuated curves contrasts with the pinched up nose and eyes and ornaments set in appliqué.

Terracotta, 19 cm. high
Date : c. 3000-2000 B.C.

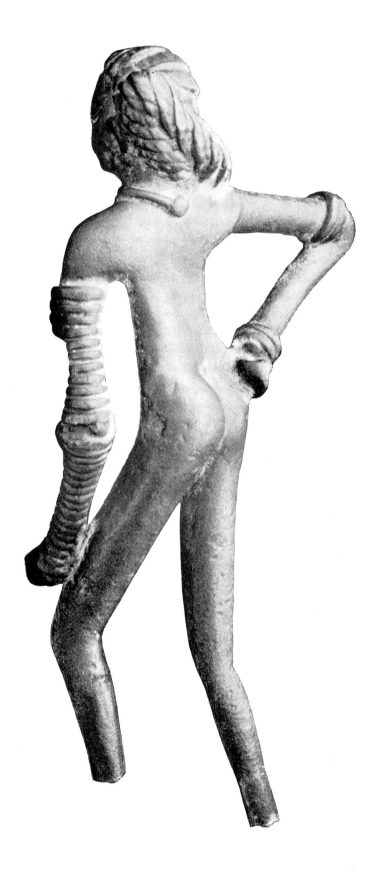

7 LEFT
DANCING GIRL, Mohenjo-daro, Sind
Bronze, 9 cm. high
Date : c. 3000-2000 B.C.
Location : Archaeological Museum,
Mohenjo-daro
One of the earliest specimens of ciré-perdue
casting in India. Represents another facet
of the Indus valley tradition.

9 RIGHT
BULL CAPITAL,
Rampurva, Bihar
Sandstone, 202·5 cm. high
Date : 322-185 B.C.
Location :
National Museum, New
Delhi
A monolithic capital of
highly polished surface.
It portrays the traditional
Indian bull with all its
restrained vigour and
dignity. The stone
beneath the body is
uncut.

8 ABOVE   Date : c. 800 B.C.
NUDE, Lauriya-Nandangarh, Bihar   Location : Indian Museum, Calcutta
Embossed gold leaf, 2·5 cm. high.
Found in a burial casket, this nude, probably the earth goddess, serves as a link
between the art of the Indus valley and that of the Gangetic. The figurine,
a complete work, reminds one of the Vedic concept of the units of measurement—
8 paramanus (the infinitesimally small particles of cosmic dust, i e. atom)
=1 rajas, 8 rajamsi=1 balagra (hair's end), and so on, up to 1 angula (a finger's
breadth)—the measurement with which image-making was started.

10
YAKSHI, Didarganj, Bihar
Sandstone, 160 cm. high
Date : c. 2nd century B.C.

Location : National Museum,
New Delhi

Suggesting a long established tradition this superb figure of the Yakshi, massive and sensuous, has no other Indian parallel in spirit or execution. With firm legs, curving hips, a long back, a narrow waist and a deeply hollowed navel, and with solid but resilient, strong and adult bosoms and belly, broad shoulders and a luminous facial expression she is the very embodiment of classical beauty.

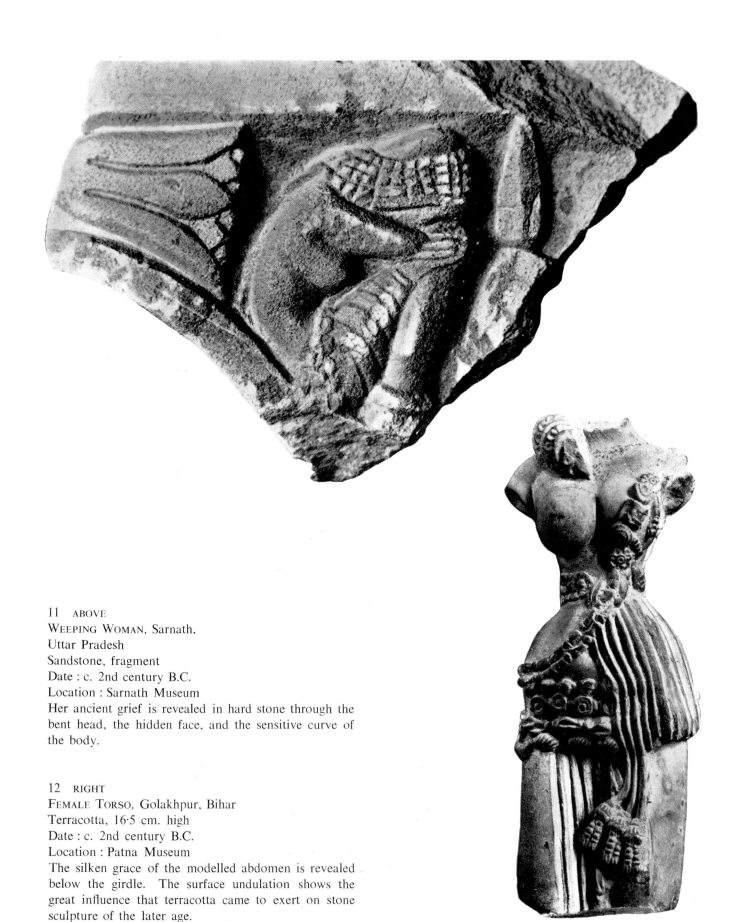

11 ABOVE
WEEPING WOMAN, Sarnath,
Uttar Pradesh
Sandstone, fragment
Date : c. 2nd century B.C.
Location : Sarnath Museum
Her ancient grief is revealed in hard stone through the
bent head, the hidden face, and the sensitive curve of
the body.

12 RIGHT
FEMALE TORSO, Golakhpur, Bihar
Terracotta, 16·5 cm. high
Date : c. 2nd century B.C.
Location : Patna Museum
The silken grace of the modelled abdomen is revealed
below the girdle. The surface undulation shows the
great influence that terracotta came to exert on stone
sculpture of the later age.

13

FIGURINE, Patna, Bihar

Terracotta, 28·5 cm. high

Date : c. 2nd century B.C.

Location : Patna Museum

Probably represents a court damsel. The highly ornate head-dress, sensitive face, panniered skirt and well modelled limbs mark an advance in the clay modeller's art in ancient India. The face is moulded. The armlets, jewellery and details of the head-dress are in appliqué.

14

KUVERA YAKSHA, Bharhut, Madhya Bharat   Date : 185-80 B.C.
Red sandstone, 212 cm. high   Location : Indian Museum, Calcutta
With folded hands the massive Yaksha figure reveals the primitive vigour
characteristic of the art of Bharhut. The partly visible contour of Sudarsana Yakshi
standing at right angle has the same quality.

15 RIGHT
MAYA'S DREAM (railing medallion),
Bharhut, Madhya Bharat
Red sandstone, 51 cm. high
Date : 185-80 B.C.
Location : Indian Museum, Calcutta
Maya was to become the mother of
the Buddha. One night she dreamt of
a majestic white elephant entering her
womb—the Great Being was conceived

16 LEFT
MAKARA (railing medallion), Bharhut,
Madhya Bharat
Red sandstone, 51 cm. high
Date : 185-80 B.C.
Location : Indian Museum, Calcutta
The mythical aquatic animal Makara
is a symbol that assumed a variety of
forms in India and abroad. Venerated
as a divine vehicle, the Indian Makara
symbolizes the very embodiment of
the "breath of life", whose nature
can only be comprehended by estab-
lishing its connection with whirlpool—
the emphasis being obvious on its
spirally curled and composite body
structure. The low relief with the
prominently carved contour suggests
the influence of wood technique.
Sculpture in wood must have been
practised for centuries before stone
came into play.

17
GODDESS OF LOVE, Mathura(?)
Ivory, 24 cm. high
Date : c. 1st century B.C.
Location : National Museum,
Naples, Italy
Recovered from Pompeii, the ivory
figure has been identified by some as
the Indian goddess of love in the
Mathura style. The concentration on
toilet by her two attendants suggests
that it was originally intended to be
the handle of a mirror.

18 RIGHT   Sandstone, detail
GATEWAY   Date : 70-25 B.C.
Location : East Gate, Stupa No. 1, Sanchi, Bhopal
Popular art found expression in stone in the service of Buddhism, much being
borrowed from the technique of the ivory carver. The method of continuous
narration was employed for a story-telling effect. Serving as a bracket in the
scheme of decoration at Sanchi gateways, the dryad seems to be an ideal female
form as conceived in India during that age.

20 ABOVE
HEAD, Sarnath, Uttar Pradesh
Sandstone, 15 cm. high
Date : c. 100 B.C.
Location : Sarnath Museum
Probably a donor's portrait, with wide eyes, heavy lips and long, curly moustache.
The head has an expression of massive quality.   The surface of the stone is highly
polished.

19   FACING PAGE
CHAITYA-VERANDAH
Rock-cut, façade

Date : Late 1st century B.C.
Location : Karli, Bombay

The façade, chiselled out of stone in the nature of wooden ribs, offers a perfect
equilibrium of design and dimension from every angle, and each carving or opening
is relevant to it.   The general mass is rather ponderous but contrivances have
been used to counteract that effect.   The figures, niches and double-carved arches
create an impression of upward thrust and mobility.

21
BUDDHA AND THE MUST ELEPHANT,
Stupa No. 1, Amaravati, Madras
Grey marble, 80 cm. high
Date : 150-300 A.D.
Location : Government Museum, Madras
Three attempts were made to kill Buddha, mainly by Devadatta, his cousin.
Here the must elephant Nalagiri, sent for the purpose, enters through the
gate trampling down the citizens, who get panicky, and throwing off with his
trunk whoever comes in his way. Women on the balcony watch the scene in
silent horror. The elephant then reaches Buddha, only to bow down before the
Master in meek submission.

22
YAKSHI, Mathura,
Uttar Pradesh
Red sandstone,
129 cm. high
Date : 2nd century A.D.
Location : National
Museum, New Delhi
The girl carries the bird
cage, while the parrot
pecks her hair resting on
her left arm. She looks
nude but a ridge across
her feet indicates a dia-
phanous muslin skirt. The
significance of the dwarf
on which she stands is
not definitely known.
The balcony above her
head shows two women
engaged in toilet.

23
THE GOOSE GIRL, Begram,
Afghanistan
Ivory, 7·5 × 6·5 cm.
Date : c. 200 A.D.
Location : Kabul Museum
Following in the tradition of Mathura, a group of artists, probably migrating from
India, founded the great art centre near Kabul. They were not only masters
in shaping ivory but were equally efficient in carving rock boulders into images
of colossal dimension.

24

HEAD, Taxila, Punjab
Stucco, 27 cm. high
Date : 2nd-3rd century A.D.
Location : Central Asian Antiquities Museum, New Delhi
Inspired primarily by Hellenistic influence, the art of Gandhara evolved
into a vigorous local Indian school. The face has a charming
innocence, and the luxuriant hair, the large, gentle eyes, the well shaped
nose and the thin but firm chin have added to the warmth of expression.

25 LEFT
BODHISATTVA, Sanchi, Bhopal
Red sandstone, 87 cm. high
Date : 5th century A.D.
Location : Victoria and Albert Museum,
London
The torso of a Bodhisattva is perhaps the
finest specimen of classical sculpture. The
delicately carved necklace, shoulder strap
and drapery and the band round the waist
serve to bring out the superb symmetry of
the idealized body.

26 RIGHT
BUDDHA, Mathura, Uttar Pradesh
Red sandstone, 217 cm. high
Date : 320-500 A.D.
Location : National Museum, New Delhi
Standing in benign majesty Buddha asks the
world not to fear. The right hand, suggesting the Abhaya pose, is broken. The rich
decoration of the nimbus has a delicate
beauty. The schematic folds of the trans-
parent cloak, under which the form is
charmingly revealed, magnify the height.

27, 28
FLYING GANDHARVAS
Mural ; detail
Date : 320-500 A.D.
Location : Cave XVII, Ajanta, Hyderabad-Dn.
In this scene depicting Gandharvas, Apsaras and the god Indra, the Vakataka-Gupta art has reached its zenith. In lively red, green, yellow and black, derived mainly from rock and vegetable sources, the artist has created wonders in depth and dimension. With his sensuous grasp of form and colour, he uses skilful gradations of tone, giving the effect of volume through light and shade.

29
FIGHTING BULLS
Mural ; detail
Date : 600 A.D.
Location : Cave No. I, Ajanta, Hyderabad-Dn.
A masterpiece of animal study in the later Gupta style. Working in light reflected through a white muslin placed outside the large, dark halls, the guild artist of Ajanta expressed new ideas in methods and techniques handed down from generation to generation.

30

LADY WITH THE LOTUS

Mural ; detail

Date : c. 479-497 A.D.

Location : Sigiriya, Ceylon

The figure in profile with a blossoming flower in one hand and a long-stemmed water-lily between two lotuses in the other has no religious significance. According to some, it is the portrait of a lady of the court of king Kasyapa I. In simple colours, the work is executed with a surprising purity of line.

31 ABOVE
PARVATI, Ahichchhtra, Uttar Pradesh
Terracotta ; 12 cm. high
Date : 500 A.D.
Location : National Museum, New Delhi
With heavy eyelids, drooping lower lips, full, fleshy face and
beautifully tufted hair, the head of Parvati reveals the ideal of feminine
beauty at that age.

32 RIGHT
SIVA, Ahichchhtra, Uttar Pradesh
Terracotta ; 19 cm. high
Date : 500 A.D.
Location : National Museum, New Delhi
The technical angularities of this terracotta head must have been an
inspiring example to those who worked in stone.

33
KISS
Rock-hewn
Date : 600-850 A.D.
Location : Kailasa
Temple,
Elura, Hyderabad-Dn.
The spirit that has
survived the ravages of
time. This union of
the male and female
figures, carved in deep
relief, is a symbol of
eternal consummation.
His arms are round
her waist while hers
are thrown across his
chest ; he is erect
and motionless as if he
has possessed her in
the darkest and most
secret depths of her
being.

34
COLUMNS
Rock-hewn
Date : 600-850 A.D.
Location : Indra Sabha Cave, Elura, Hyderabad-Dn.
Under the chisel of the artists in India even rocks flowered into beautiful forms of architecture. The columns were evolved beyond their utilitarian purpose with decorative ornaments of endless variety and grace.

35
DESCENT OF THE GANGES
Rock-hewn, detail
Date : 600-750 A.D.
Location : Mahabalipuram, Madras
The artists, undaunted by the unwieldy material, brave the bare rock extending over a wide area and create an extremely lyrical frieze, full of movement, on the epic subject of the Gangavatarana. Bhagiratha is represented as worshipping Siva, seen in relief in front of the door of the shrine. The deer, part of the same scene, are evidence of the heights which animal sculpture in India achieved.

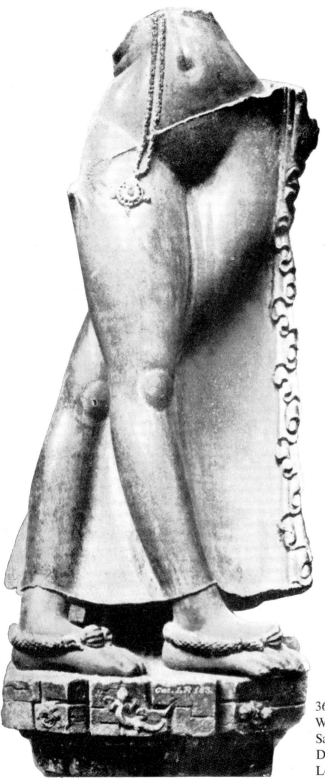

36
WOMAN, Madhya Pradesh (?)
Sandstone, 89 cm. high
Date : 6-7th century A.D.
Location : National Museum,
New Delhi

A fragment from the waist downwards of a woman painted red. Her legs are long
and straight, but just above the knees her thighs begin to swell out round and solid,
broadening gradually to her hips from which a waist cloth suspends. Her belly
has a fluent, down-slipping grace. The figure stands on a cornice, on which a
lizard is carved.

37
WOMAN WITH A PARROT,
Rajmahal, Bihar
Whitish sandstone,
81·5 cm. high
Date : 6-7th century A.D.
Location : National
Museum, New Delhi
The figure is carved in
deep relief between two
rosette-borders on a door-
jamb. She appears to be
feeding with right hand
a parrot at her feet. From
the upper parts of her
arms a scarf hangs up to
her ankles. A skirt
protects the groin and
belly but the breasts are
bare.

38, 39 PART VIEW
MAHESA
Rock-hewn, 360 cm. high
Date : 8th century A.D.

Location : Elephanta, Bombay
Deep in a niche, the three-headed Mahesa in meditation suggests
mystery and power, symbolizing 'the union of one's inner self
with the cosmic world.

40
SUJATA'S OFFERING
Dark grey stone, detail
Date : c. 750 A.D.
Location : Borobudur, Java
To seek a way out of suffering and death for mankind, Prince Siddhartha, the future Buddha, left his home, and spent long years in intense meditation. At the end of this penance, he received his first morsel of food from Sujata, daughter of an outcast. A pitted volcanic rock, a most unsympathetic material, was transformed into scenes revealing a moving story. The lower galleries are lined with panels of bas-relief sculptures, illustrating stories from the life of Buddha.

41, 42
SUDHANA AT THE FOUNTAIN
Dark grey stone, detail
Date : c. 750 A.D.
Location : Gallery I, Borobudur, Java
This is the famous Jataka, in which Prince Sudhana is casting his ring into the
water-pot of one of the Kinnaris at the fountain ; the other Kinnaris are returning
home carrying their pitchers. It has been estimated that if all the sculpture panels
of Borobudur are placed end to end it would be over 5 kilometres long.

44 RIGHT
DANCING APSARA, Tra-kieu, Champa
Grey sandstone, detail
Date : 8-9th century A.D.
Location : Archaeological Museum, Tourane, Indo-China
Reflects the style of the Indian Gupta Period. The enigmatic smile, and the
rhythmic movement of the figure blend into an attitude of ultimate devotion
and surrender.

43 FACING PAGE
SIVA
Black stone, fragment
Date : 9th century A.D.
Location : Vishnu Temple, Prambanam, Java
The skull on the crown of the enormous head of Siva contrasts with the serene
expression of the face. The contrast is heightened by the third eye, set vertically
on the forehead, which is symbolical of divine insight.

45 LEFT
WATER-NYMPH
Mural, detail
Date : c. 8th century A.D.
Location : Dandan U'iliq, Central Asia
Central Asia was the fusion ground of different influences from great civilizations around. Indian influence was most marked in murals and stucco figures.

46 RIGHT
BODHISATTVA
Mural, detail
Date : c. 8th century A.D.
Location : Horyuji Temple, Nara, Japan
The murals on the Kondo (Golden Hall) of Horyuji temple suggests that Indian artists took part in the execution of these paintings. A disastrous fire destroyed these in January 1949.

47

APSARA, Isvarapura Temple, Bonteai-Sri, Cambodia
Sandstone, detail
Date : c. 967 A.D.
Location : Musée Guimet, Paris
With the massive contour of the head and the sturdy neck, the figure pulsates with
life. The coiffure and the pendulating ear-rings are highly stylized.

48, 49 TWO VIEWS
GOMMATESVARA
Stone, 17·38 metre high
Date : 10th century A.D.
Location : Sravana Belgola, Mysore
This nude colossus, the biggest monolithic statue in the world, stands as a great
sentinel, majestic and severe, between the earth and the sky and shows outstanding
comprehension of the form and volume of the human body.

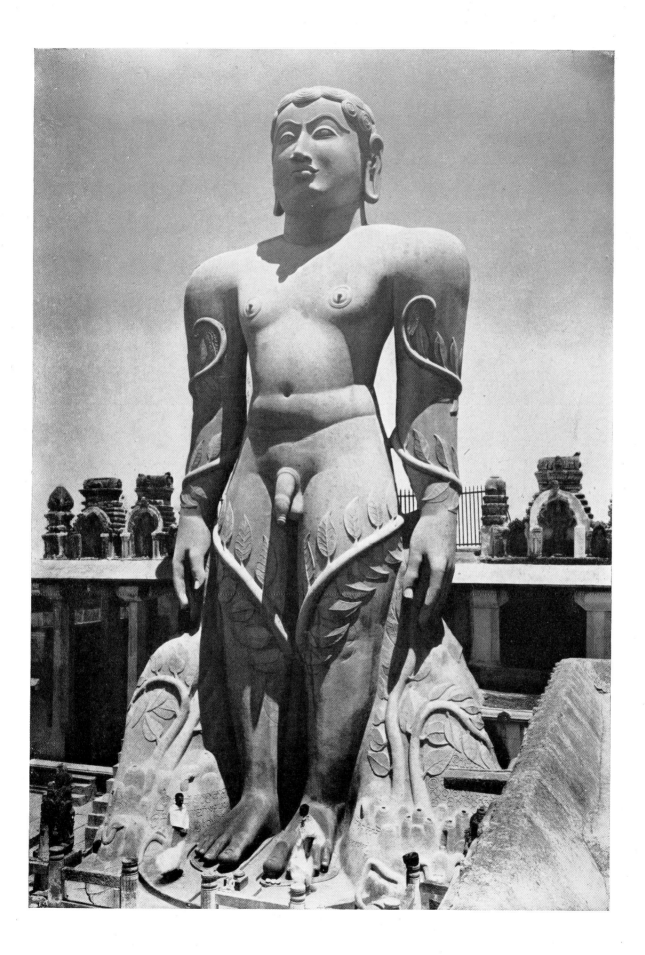

50, 51 TWO VIEWS
TORANA
Sandstone
Date : c. 950 A.D.
Location : Muktesvara Temple, Bhubanesvara, Orissa
A singular architectural triumph of the ancient Hindu in the construction of archway.
The heavy rectangular shadow and the massive supports give an effect of solidity,
which, however, is counteracted by the decorative motifs executed in such a way
that the eye can follow the details without any strain.

52 LEFT
GABAKSHA
Sandstone, detail
Date : c. 950 A.D.
Location : Muktesvara Temple, Bhubanesvara,
Orissa
A combination of ornamental designs with human
and animal figures, with the stress on pure patterns.

53 BELOW
LINGARAJA TEMPLE
Sandstone, 43·2 metre
Date : c. 1000 A.D.
Location : Bhubanesvara, Orissa
A tremendous force seems to drive the structure
upwards, creating an impression of movement in
space.

54

NATARAJA, Tiruvelangadu, Madras
Bronze, 114·5 cm. high
Date : 11th century A.D.

Location : Government Museum,
Madras

Siva, engaged in the dance of the universe, tramples on the dwarf of illusion, holding the drum of creation in the upper right hand and the fire of destruction in the corresponding left. The lower right hand is stretched out in a gesture of abhaya—protection—and the lower left signifies salvation. The outer circle of fire symbolizes the universe. A unique blend of poise and movement, this sculpture is remarkable for the balance of the limbs and the rhythm running through them.

55 ABOVE
MOTHER AND CHILD, Khajuraho, Madhya Bharat
Sandstone, full figure 92 cm. high
Date : 11th century A.D.
Location : National Museum, New Delhi
This figure and No. 58, so long thought to be from Bhubanesvara, really belong, as Dr. Kramrisch has pointed out, to the Khajuraho group of sculptures. For a proper appreciation of these figures, one has to relate them to the temples of which they formed part.

56 RIGHT
KANDARIYA MAHADEVA TEMPLE
Sandstone
Date : c. 950-1050 A.D.
Location : Khajuraho, Madhya Bharat
The horizontal stability of the base balances the extreme vertical mobility of the sikhara. The massive groupings are intersected by the main lines and shadow patterns, giving the whole c o m p o s i t i o n an air of organic strength and enabling the eye to take in the whole structure at a single glance. The temple is 'all base and all roof', a pure monument.

57 FACING PAGE
KANDARIYA MAHADEVA TEMPLE
Sandstone, detail
Date : c. 950-1050 A.D.
Location : Khajuraho, Madhya Bharat
The base is crowded with diverse figures,
but inside the temple where one meditates
it is plain and dark—Garbhagriha—the
darkness of the womb.

58   RIGHT
TOILET, Khajuraho, Madhya Bharat
Sandstone, 95·5 cm. high
Date : 11th century A.D.
Location : National Museum, New Delhi
The woman, under a tree, is engaged in
toilet, holding a mirror in her left hand and
with her right putting vermilion at the
parting of the hair. Two attendants, one a
woman wearing a satchel, and the other,
a man, carrying a bag, stand on either side.

59
MITHUNA AND THE MAIDENS
Sandstone, detail
Date : 1059-1087 A.D.
Location : Visvanatha Temple, south wall,
Khajuraho, Madhya Bharat
This particular bandha or pose of the union (mithuna) of
man and woman is a masterly depiction of the spirit of
physical absorption through the medium of stone. The
implication of these figures occurring at the lower ridges of
Indian temples is that, before one can be initiated into the life
of a devotee, one must go through all earthly pleasures,
including the raptures of the body, which is considered
the temple of god.

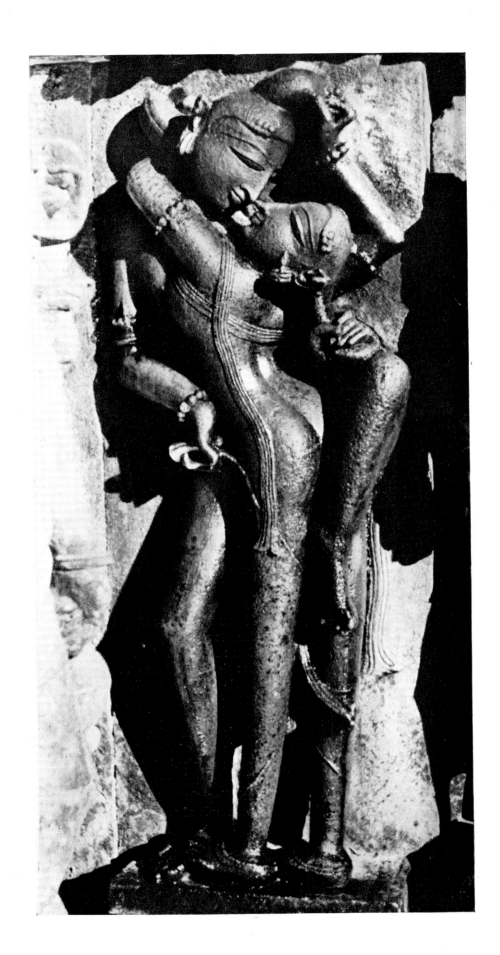

60 FACING PAGE
MITHUNA
Sandstone, 60 × 180 cm.
Date : c. 1059-1087 A.D.
Location : Jagadamba
Temple, south wall,
Khajuraho, Madhya Bharat
The expression of rapture
of the faces of the couple
lends a tender quality to
the stone figures. The slip-
ping hem of the loin cloth,
undone by the lover, the
twisted hair and the movement of the fingers, all
combine to convey the effect
of an utter surrender by the
woman.

61 ABOVE
HEAD OF A QUEEN (?), Dinajpur, Bengal
Blackstone, 18·4 cm. high
Date : 10-11th century A.D.
Location : Asutosh Museum, Calcutta
This has all the delicate qualities of painting which, in the medieval
period, came to generate ideas for sculpture. The features suggest a
portrait head.

63
LION BRACKET,
Khajuraho, Madhya Bharat
Sandstone, 108 cm. high
Date : 11th century A.D.
Location : National
Museum, New Delhi
The treatment of the lion,
whose human rider is so
small as to be almost
invisible, is highly stylized.
The left hind leg of the
beast is about to come
down on a warrior, whose
twisted body suggests a
final, desperate movement
to defend himself.

62   FACING PAGE
GANGA, Rajsahi, Bengal
Blackstone, detail
Date : 12th century A.D.
Location : V. R. S. Museum,
Rajsahi.
In elaborate attire and
costly ornaments this figure,
though represented as a
goddess, can very well be
the portrait of a full-
blooded woman of that age.

64, 65

JAGAMOHANA

Sandstone, 261·18 × 173·73 metre

Date : 1240-1280 A.D.

Location : Surya Temple, Konarak, Orissa

Dedicated to the Sun-God Arka, the giver of life, this famous temple is in the form
of a huge chariot. From a distance the eye is tilted to embrace it ; then caught
by a succession of structural lines and ultimately brought to rest by the circular
amlaka and the base—a pure composition which is rare in Indian architecture.
Each wheel has eight spokes, asta-prahar, or the traditional division of day and
night into eight periods. The symbolic figures on the spokes appear to be in motion
as one moves from one wheel to another. The part of the chariot that has survived
carries the Jagamohana—Fascinator of the Universe. From the base of the temple
to the top is depicted life in all its variety and immensity—the Upanishadic 'prano
virat'. No phase of life, including the sensual, is ignored ; there is no taboo and
everything contributes to the total picture.

66 ABOVE
MUSICIAN   Sandstone, detail
Location : Surya Temple,   Date : 1240-1280 A.D.
Konarak, Orissa
Placed high up on successive pyramidal tiers, these bold and gay
musicians show that religion did not inhibit the Indian artist.

67 RIGHT
SURYA
Chlorite, 240 cm. high
Date : 1240-1280 A.D.
Location : Surya Temple,
Konarak, Orissa
The sun-god has on his
right side Dandin, the
dispenser of justice holding a sword, and on the
left, Pingala, the recorder
of the human deeds, with
pen and inkpot in hand.

68

MITHUNA
Sandstone, detail
Date : 1240-1280 A.D.

Location: Surya Temple,
Konarak, Orissa

The interlocked figures, rendered with a rare combination of monumental and mobile qualities, breathe of flesh and feeling and through convulsed curves, portray the desire for a total sinking of the selves at the moment of mating. But the whole impression makes one forget the real theme and suggests the idea of some mysterious, underlying purpose. A close-up of the face appears on the jacket of this book.

69   FACING PAGE

ELEPHANT AND THE WARRIOR
Sandstone
Date : 1240-1280 A.D.
Location : Surya Temple, north gate,
Konarak, Orissa
The elephant carries a warrior in his trunk.
Full of sympathy and affection, this study of animal
life reminds of the spirit that inspired the early
sculptures of Bharhut and Sanchi.

70   RIGHT

ARDHANARISVARA, Vikrampur, Bengal
Black stone
Date : c. 12th century A.D.
Location : Dacca Museum, Bengal
The male and female attributes are shown as part
of the same body, thus anticipating a much later
discovery. This medieval anthropomorphic form
develops from the timeless icon of linga-joni
signifying Purusha and Prakriti, the expression of
which in abstract form is to be found in the
uncarved stones on Page 38. They are symbols
of primal creation and, united, they become the
most powerful force unfolding divergent aspects
of the cosmic reality.

71 ABOVE
VISHNU AND ATTENDANT, Sundarban, 24 Parganas, Bengal
Engraving on copper plate, 20·5 × 27 cm.
Date : 1198 A.D.
Location : Asutosh Museum, Calcutta
A land grant inscription with silver coating bearing the name of King Dommanapala.
The lines, with their lyrical grace, approximate to the trend of medieval painting.
The style greatly influenced art in South-East Asia, particularly Indonesia.

72 UPPER RIGHT
SCENE FROM THE JATAKAS
Mural, detail
Date : c. 13th century A.D.
Location : Payathonzu Temple,
Pagan, Burma
The nervous outline of these murals
has stylistic affinities with the medieval
paintings of Bengal. Their charac-
teristic features are the three-quarter
face with elongated eyes and nose.

73 LOWER RIGHT
SCENE FROM THE DEVADHARMA JATAKA
Engraving on stone
Date : c. 1361 A.D.
Location : Wat Si Jum, Sukhodaya,
Siam
The engraving, an outline drawing on
stone, has no typical Siamese flavour ;
on the contrary, it has strong affinities
with the late medieval Indian and
Ceylonese murals depicting Jataka
stories.

74
CEILING
White marble, detail
Date : 1232 A.D.
Location : Tejapala Temple, Dilwara, Mount Abu
The ceiling of the temple, standing 4,000 feet above the sea-level, shows the conception of the mandala, the concentric circles. The total effect has been marred by the exuberance of the carvings, which were done by scraping and not by chipping.

75

MADANIKA

Stone

Date : 12th century A.D.

Location : Chenna Kesava Temple, Belur, Mysore

A pure pattern executed in minute detail. In this figure bracket, one of the thirty-eight that decorate the capitals of the pillars, the ornaments streamline the rhythm of the human body.

76 BACK VIEW   Date : 14-15th century A.D.
KRISHNA   Location : Somnath Temple, Dungarpur, Rajputana
Stone
Following the technique of the wood-carver, the sculptor has brought out in a
striking manner the contours of the human form.

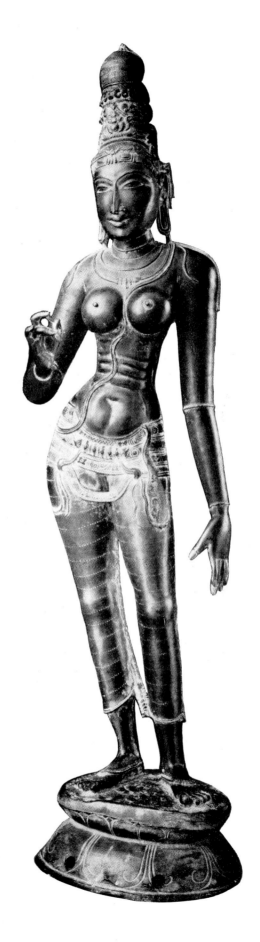

77 FACING PAGE
KUTB MINAR
Stone, 72 metre high
Date : 13th century A.D.
The sudden incongruity of the Kutb against a
bleak background has been compensated by the
arabesque ornaments and the deep shadows
created by the flutings.

78   RIGHT
PARVATI, Tanjore, Madras
Bronze, 92 cm. high
Date : 15th century A.D.
Location : National Museum, New Delhi
Parvati standing on a lotus pedestal. The hair is
tied into a high bun, and the waist modelled with
four deep crossfolds.

79, 80
BIRTH AND TONSURE OF MAHAVIRA, Western India
Painting on paper, 25 cm. × 7·7 cm.
Date : 1439 A.D.
Location : National Museum, New Delhi
The almond-shaped and somewhat protruding eyes bespeak the influence of
sculpture on painting, resulting in an attempt to create a three-dimensional effect
on two-dimensional space ; but the brutal absence of any softening shadows makes
the painting essentially of a flat nature.

81
ELOPEMENT AT NIGHT, Western India
Painting on paper, 21·5 cm. × 12 cm.

Date : 16th century A.D.
Location : Bharat Kala Bhawan, Banaras

The invigorating folk element is present in the bold and sharp outlines, the
different parts merging into a rhythm of movement.

82　ABOVE
HUMAYUN'S TOMB
Red sandstone and white marble
Date : c. 1560 A.D.
Location : Delhi
The mausoleum has a sombre dignity that is
heightened by the use of red sandstone and
white marble inlaid on the surface broken by
arches. Placed within a planned garden the tomb
breathes an air of purity, classic peace and eternal
stability.

83　RIGHT
PANCH-MAHAL
Red sandstone
Date : 16th century A.D.
Location : Fatehpur Sikri, Uttar Pradesh
This five-storied pavilion of Akbar's time is an
example of how Hindu and Islamic craftsmanship fused in India. The ground floor adorned
profusely by vigorous columns was sub-divided
into thin screens of stone, some perforated,
some solid.

84
SCREEN
White marble
Date : 1628-1656 A.D.
Location : Taj Mahal, Agra, Uttar Pradesh
The perforated screens with lapidary work and
pietra-dura inlay on the cenotaph of the Taj
relieve the cold air of the tomb and add a
lyrical grace.

85
SIVA AND PARVATI, Nepal
Bronze, detail
Date : c. 15th century A.D.
Location unknown
The ciré-perdue method is here employed to show Siva and his wife in yab-yum
or complete unison. Though intensely alive, the figures show great restraint
and refinement.

86

PARVATI, South India   Date : c. 17th century A.D.

Bronze, 42 cm. high   Location : National Museum, New Delhi

Parvati, otherwise known as Sakti or Creative Energy, is represented here in severe
outline. The hair, dressed high, bears a crescent moon. Behind the head there
is a large disc for hanging garlands.

87
GOPURAM
Masonry below, brick and stucco above
Date : 17th century A.D.
Location: Minakshi Temple, Madura, Madras
Built on many planes upwards, the structure has unity, totality and continuity,
but the multitudinous images and intricate ornamental designs tend to counteract
and disintegrate that effect.

88 ABOVE
GOPIS IN ARBOUR, Nayagarh, Orissa
Painting on paper, 20·5 × 32 cm.
Date : Late 17th century A.D.
Location : Asutosh Museum, Calcutta
The agitated lines in which the human and
animal figures have been painted bring out the
emotional aspect of waiting for Krishna by the
milkmaids. A masterpiece of Orissa tradition.

89 RIGHT
NAYIKA, Kangra, Himachal Pradesh
Pahari painting on paper
Date : 18th century A.D.
Location : National Museum, New Delhi
Part of the Rajput tradition, the Kangra paintings, mainly page-size representations of stories
from popular mythology, excel in warm colours
—lemon yellow, dark blue, olive green, tomato
red, chalk white and gold. This figure portrays
frustration in love.

90
POLO
Mughal painting on paper, 30 cm. × 20 cm.
Date: 18th century A.D.
Location: National Museum, New Delhi
A fine miniaturist of the Mughal court brings out the quick movement of polo—the
favourite game of the emperors—against a carefully composed landscape.

91
LOVERS IN A GROVE
Mughal painting on paper
Date: 17th century A.D.
Location: National Museum, New Delhi
The portrait-like figures, placed in the centre of a broad, foliate frame, and the
idealized trees, mountains and clouds, combine the refinements of the Mughal and
Rajput schools of painting.

92
RADHA AND KRISHNA, Kangra, Himachal Pradesh
Pahari painting on paper
Date : 18th century A.D.
Location : Lucknow Museum, Uttar Pradesh
The theme is Hindu but the treatment Mughal.
Refugee painters from the plains who settled in
the Himalayan region dwelt on various aspects
of emotion mainly through the Radha-Krishna
love theme.

93
COUPLE, Ganjam, Orissa
Painting on paper, 12·5 cm. × 11·5 cm.
Date : 19th century A.D.
Location : D. P. Ghosh's collection, Calcutta
Painting in Orissa emulates the sharp, edgy
lines of the murals in Elura, achieving a three-
dimensional effect on a flat surface. The virility is
noteworthy.

94
KRISHNALILA, Midnapore, Bengal
Scroll-painting on paper, 52·5 cm. × 75 cm.
Date : 19th century A.D.
Location : Asutosh Museum, Calcutta
The patuas of Bengal deal with a wide range of themes, including the popular mythological stories. Their paintings appeal directly to the eye, without any kind of subterfuge or detour, avoiding the vague fantasy which had been evolved in Indian iconography and which had led to the betrayal of fundamental form. Moreover, the pata-paintings are a collective creation, the team-work of several members of a family, with innovations and discoveries behind them by generations.

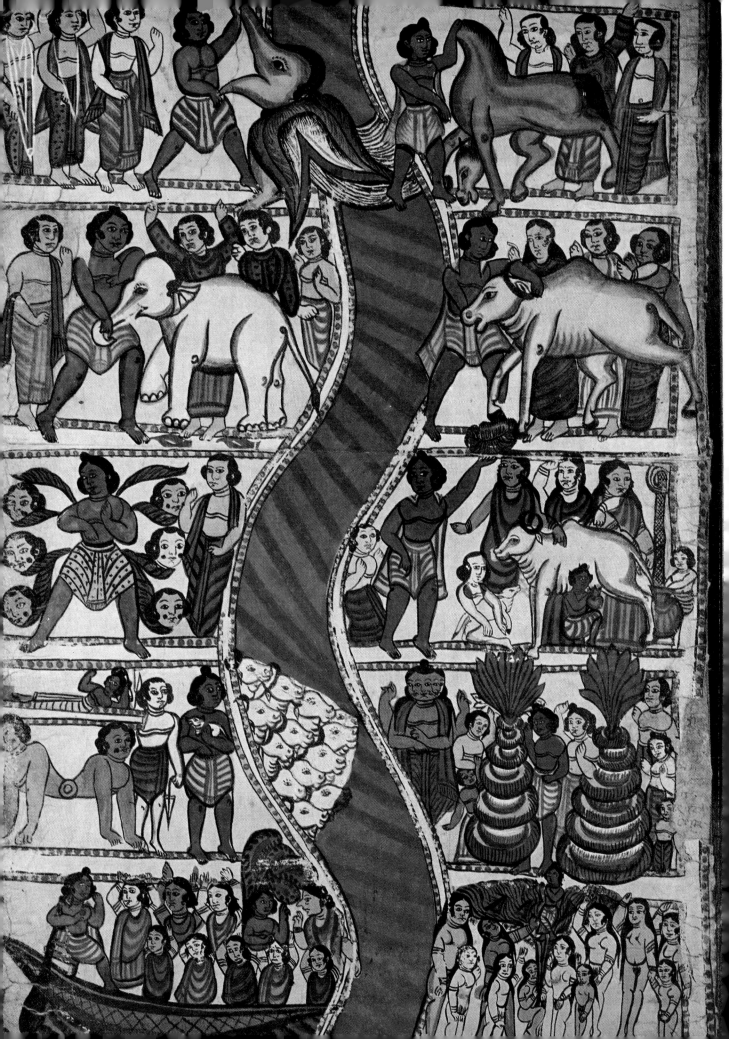

95
WOMAN, Goalpara, Assam
Painting on pith, 35 cm. × 15 cm.
Date : 20th century A.D.
Location : Asutosh Museum, Calcutta
The folk artist creates his form with the minimum
effort through bold lines and pure colours.

96
MAN THINKING
Wood
Date : 20th century A.D.
Location : Indian Tribal Research Unit's collection
Wood appeals to the tribals in India as a suitable
medium. This figure, very simple in character,
represents the basic outline of human form, but
there is an attempt at naturalization in the hair,
which has been affixed.

97
A NEGLECTED WIFE
Kalighat, Calcutta
Painting on paper

Date: Early 20th century A.D.
Location: Late D. C. Sen's collection, Calcutta

A neglected wife falls asleep after waiting for her Westernized husband, who is out boozing. In the hands of the Kalighat patuas, who revolted from the idealistic view of life, art became a powerful instrument of satire and a form of revenge for social injustice. A line drawing of the same theme is on the frontispiece.

98

Date: Early 20th century A.D.

KACHA AND DEVAYANI

Location: Indian Museum, Calcutta

Fresco by Abanindranath Tagore

Abanindranath looked beyond his time and liberally received inspiration from sources of widely varying nature. Of his few experiments in technique other than water-colour, Kacha-o-Devayani is an outstanding example of fresco work.

99
THE FAWN
Water-colour by Rabindranath Tagore
Date : 20th century A.D.
Location unknown
The poet-painter draws his lines with a sure hand and the spacing is so accurate as is only possible from the most experienced artists with years of practice behind them.

100   Date : 20th century A.D.
BIRTH OF THE BUDDHA   Location : National Museum, New Delhi
Tempera by Nandalal Bose
Nandalal, the foremost disciple of Abanindranath, has been much influenced by the Indian classical art and the murals of Ajanta have a firm grip on him. Though like a miniature, the painting has all the qualities of a mural.

101
HEAD
Tempera by Jamini Roy
Date : 20th century A.D.
Location : Author's collection
In his exploration in the field of forms Jamini Roy
breaks new grounds. A work of the earlier phase
of his new quest, bold in colour and simple in
execution.

102
MOTHER AND CHILD, 24 Parganas, Bengal
Painted clay, 10·2 cm. high
Date : 20th century A.D.
Location : Asutosh Museum, Calcutta
This folk doll painted in yellow and vermilion
mixed with milk is a remarkable variation on the
ever recurring theme of mother and child. The
rhythm of the composition reveals an economy
which is reminiscent of modernistic sculpture.

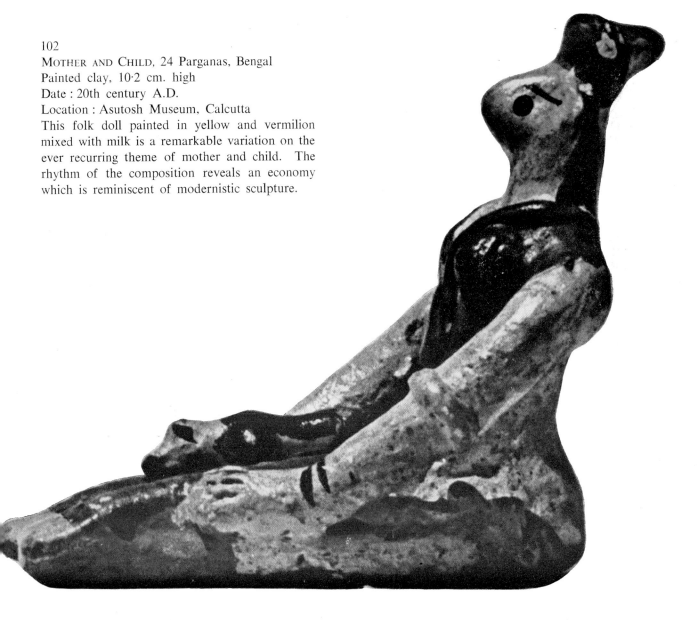